LIVING TRADITIONS

INTERIORS BY
MATTHEW PATRICK SMYTH

LIVING
TRADITIONS
INTERIORS BY
MATTHEW PATRICK SMYTH

PRINCIPAL PHOTOGRAPHY BY JOHN GRUEN
WRITTEN WITH JUDITH NASATIR

I would like to dedicate this book to my clients, who have given me their loyal support over the years. I've been very lucky to have had only "nice" clients, which makes a world of difference! If I were to do a family tree of clients it would stem back to my friends Tony Korner and Eugenie Voorhees. Thank you for believing in me so early on.

To the magazine editors, writers, and photographers who have helped promote my work over the years. Without their help, there would be no book.

In memory of Alvin Karstensen, George O'Brien, Billy Goldsmith, Bob Menhennett, and my Mother. They all set the course.

Finally, and above all, to Jean Vallier for 28 years of listening to me worry but never hearing a word!

TABLE OF CONTENTS

INTRODUCTION

So much of my life has come neatly full circle, but my life in design came completely out of the blue. Growing up in a close-knit Irish Catholic community did not expose me to the world of design and decoration directly or indirectly. My elementary education was in the hands of nuns who taught me long division and cursive, but who never mentioned interior design or architecture—not in relation to our church's nave, apse, or altar, and certainly not as a career option. I'm fairly sure they still don't.

No one breathed a word about interior design in high school, either. And in college I bounced from major to major, from theater eventually to business, and only to please my family. When I graduated, the one sure thing I knew was that I had much more to learn. I was twenty-two years old. I was trying to make a go of commercial photography. I was a bit lost. One day, I found myself watching Katharine Hepburn on the *Dick Cavett Show*. He asked why she didn't have children. She said something along these lines: "People say you can have it all, but you can't. You're never going to get anywhere unless you narrow down what you want. If you don't, you'll get to a certain point in life and nothing will pull together."

I remember thinking: "That's it. Narrow it down." I wasn't sure whether "it" meant theater, photography, or business, but "it" started coming into focus at a dinner party one night in Stone Ridge, a small town in upstate New York where I was then living. My dinner partner told me in passing that he was a weaver, and that his current project involved

handcrafting carpets and throws for a house in Lake Forest, Illinois. He went on at length about the site, a pure, eighteenth-century-style manor house that seamlessly incorporated all the modern-day conveniences yet also had plaster moldings handcrafted by artisans using centuries-old techniques. He marveled about how the designer communicated with the artisans and craftspeople: by sketching an idea or the solution to a technical problem on the walls, drawing carpets in detail, making color samples based on the custom fabrics chosen for the rooms. This designer had filled the house with the finest Georgian furniture available—sourced and purchased in London—and summoned artisans from Italy to glaze certain rooms. I had no idea then what "glaze" meant, nor, really, much else that he mentioned. But I was moved by how he spoke, so I wrote down the designer's name: David Easton.

In those pre-Google days, finding out about a designer's work meant hunting down old copies of decorating magazines. The more I read about Easton, and about decorating, the more I thought I might have found what I had been looking for. I started tagging along with a few designer friends on their client visits and helping them with their antiques business. I then bought my first book on decorating, *The New York Times Book of Interior Design and Decoration*, by Norma Skurka. I remember eyeing it in the mall in Middletown, New York, where I had a part-time job at Biltmore Tuxedos escorting model brides down a makeshift runway while wearing the brightly colored tuxedo of the week—it was the 1970s. The cover of that book, which I still have, was so beautiful—a John Saladino apartment that I could live in happily even today on the front, and classic Mario Buatta on the back.

I soon discovered that the Fashion Institute of Technology was then considered the field's most respected school. As Parsons, formerly the "best" school, shifted toward industrial design in the late 1970s, its renowned faculty—the teachers of Mario Buatta, Angelo Donghia, Thomas Britt, and so many others—had migrated to FIT. If I could get in, I would be able to learn from such legendary teachers as Stanley Barrows, Renee Smith, Glen Boyle, and Ray Kendall.

In those days FIT held the equivalent of an open entrance exam: a portfolio review by the faculty on a specific day. I pulled together ten of my photographs, made a few sketches of my bedroom, and bought a bus ticket to New York. Students who had drawings far more detailed than mine filled the auditorium, yet many of them were turned away.

While the professors were reviewing my portfolio, they huffed and puffed and waved their hands. I thought my dream was over before it began—and that maybe I would take that flight attendant job I had just applied for after all. Then they called my name, asked me a few questions, and repaired to a corner to discuss my portfolio some more. Finally Mr. Barrows walked back over to me. "Your portfolio is weak," he said, "and nothing in it really pertains to interior design, but we see something in your photographs. You seem to have a sense of perspective, so we are going to take a chance on you."

When I got back upstate, I gave notice to my boss at Biltmore Tuxedos, a wonderful woman named Agatha Rinaldi. Agatha was an Anna Magnani type—tough, gorgeous, larger-than-life. When I told her I was leaving to study interior design, she offered that she had a cousin who was a designer—then she asked if I had heard of him, Mario Buatta! I walked her to the bookstore, and as we looked at the cover of Skurka's book together, she told me stories about growing up with him on Staten Island. Today, of course, "Mario" is like "Cher," an instantly recognizable name associated with an instantly recognizable style. He and the other designers and firms in that book—David Hicks, Joe D'Urso, Ward Bennett, Thomas Britt, David Easton, Angelo Donghia, MAC II, Kevin McNamara, Parish Hadley, Denning & Fourcade, Joseph Braswell—remain a major source of inspiration. All I knew when I first pored over that book was that interior design was going to work for me. That August I moved to Manhattan, to the student floor of the West Sixty-third Street YMCA. I focused on my studies. And I never forgot about David Easton. I had no idea I would come to know many of them personally, or that, like them, I would someday be installing a room at the Kips Bay Decorator Show House.

My senior year, the president of the Interior Design Club asked me for a list of possible guest speakers. I of course suggested Easton, he accepted, and came to FIT with slides of the very same house I had heard so much about at dinner a few years before. At the end of the lecture, the club's president introduced me to him. I asked him to review my work. Polite and kind, he made me feel as though I was on the right track. At that point in my life, the only thing I was certain about was that I had to work for him.

After David left, I noticed that he had left behind a roll of blueprints—depictions of rooms that Jim Steinmeyer, his partner, had rendered exquisitely. I asked the department head if he wanted to keep them; he said I could have them if I liked. Those sketches soon covered every inch of wall surface in my room at the YMCA. I can still see those prints, their lines and nuances, as if they were in front of me.

When graduation arrived Stanley Barrows asked if I had a preference about where I might like to work. I told him with David Easton. His reply was: "A good choice. You will learn a lot, but you won't last long." That scared me. I remember thinking: what if I go to work for him and get fired soon after? What would I do, since he was the very reason I got into design? I decided to get my feet wet in a few other offices first.

The reality of working as a designer came as a shock. I discovered that I would only be devoted to actual design 10 percent of the time. The rest, the hard and important part, was detail—running around, problem solving, organizing on a massive scale with military precision. My first job made me think I had opted for the wrong profession. My boss had an extremely tough clientele. For the sake of my résumé, I stayed a year and a half, miserable, but determined to learn.

I then moved to a young firm of seven people. It was the early 1980s, when many rental apartment buildings in Manhattan began to convert to condos or co-ops and needed model apartments and updated lobbies to entice buyers. This firm specialized in those projects, and I learned how to shepherd a job from initial design and space planning to installation—in three weeks. To decide about materials and styles, we developed scenarios and personality profiles for our "clients"—a young woman in the garment district, for instance, or a young attorney on Wall Street—a process reminiscent of what I loved about theater.

I then went to work for Billy Goldsmith, an owner of Luten Clarey Stern, a firm that produced contemporary furniture classics. One day, a friend whose best friend ran Easton's office called and said he needed to hire someone fast—and could I interview that very afternoon? It was now or never. I rushed home, put on a fresh shirt and tie, dusted off my portfolio, and ran to Easton's office. I started two weeks later.

In those days the firm was just seven in all, and David worked closely with us. He taught me how to draw, and to see what he saw. I studied hard—and not just design skills. David insisted that manners mattered, and his love of travel and his sense of generosity made a mark on me. He sent me to Paul Stuart with his credit card to buy my first tuxedo so I could take a client's daughter to a ball—the same girl whose carpets were woven by my dinner companion all those years ago. I didn't think that I would have much use for a tux, grateful though I was. Once I had it, however, more black-tie invitations arrived. Better yet, I remain close with the girl I took to the ball—and got to know her sister, too. I went to their weddings and helped decorate their first apartments.

I worked on houses, apartments, boats, and planes that were once-in-a-lifetime opportunities for an assistant. I traveled with David to Madeira to design needlepoint carpets, to Venice to create vestments for a private chapel, to London to shop for antiques, and to Paris just for the sake of it. The intense training was comparable to graduate school—sleepless nights, anxiety attacks, and all—but I loved it. During my time at David's office, I thought repeatedly about what Stanley Barrows had said. After about three years, however, I stopped worrying about being fired. I held on for six years: a firm record.

For years after I left David's office, I could hear his voice in my head, guiding me. My own has taken over now, but I never forgot the lessons. The experience of working for the best is irreplaceable, as much for what it teaches about the details of design as for the exposure it provides to the finest examples of the decorative arts, to the world, and to life. That knowledge informs every aspect of what I do now.

Even after all the places I visited, my abiding love for Paris permeates my work. Whenever I'm about to start a big project, Paris always beckons. I return to New York inspired about design. That's been true since my very first trip there. I stayed in an apartment on the Right Bank with a magnificent view of the Eiffel Tower. A friend there knew the curator from Versailles, so he arranged a lunch and a private tour of the rooms then under renovation—a real eye-opener for someone living in a sixth-floor walk-up. I was determined to return, and soon.

The French lifestyle, based on fully enjoying free time, resonated with me. Who in Paris would spend a Saturday or Sunday in the office, as we Americans so often do? I made a goal of eventually keeping an apartment there, which I achieved, ten years ago. I am never bored in Paris. Each block is different. No two buildings are alike. There's always something new, and everything is individual. There's so much style, and an appreciation for every period: Art Déco, the various Louis eras, and Directoire, to name a few. I love going to the flea market on Saturday mornings, as much for the pleasure of looking as to buy. When I'm really tempted, I find myself thinking: "Will it be worth it to ship this back?" I talk myself into saying "Yes!" far too often, of course!

Much of interior design is about saying yes while saying no—or, more accurately, narrowing down the options. Where to begin when everything is possible? Many of my younger clients feel for London what I feel for Paris and New York. When they try to convey to me how they want their homes to look, they often reach back across the Atlantic for an image of what it is that they desire from their experiences there in the past—the atmosphere of a particular hotel, or a club, some special place where they've had dinner. They remember the lighting, the intimacy, the fun.

Architecture often sets a project's mood or direction, and I don't fight it unless the architecture is truly bad. Context is key: interiors should suit their time, their place, their surroundings, and their purpose. I'm not a great proponent of "Versailles in the sky," as they say. What's more jarring than walking into a modern urban apartment building, riding the elevator up thirty-eight floors, and exiting into a palatial gilt-and-velvet-covered parlor?

Rooms are not theater sets, and design is not about making fiction come to life. Rooms should express the needs and personalities of the people who live in them, now. That's my main goal. The relationship between designer and client is like any intimate relationship: it either clicks, or it doesn't. The client makes a project successful. I need mine to be involved, to have an emotional attachment to where they live, because no one can be happy in a forced or arbitrary interior—it's just too personal.

RULES

Maybe it's because of the nuns' schooling, but rules matter to me. I've never doubted that rules exist for a reason, or that the rules are the rules because they make sense. In design, they are essential and must be taught. Right and wrong do exist in matters of planning, scale, proportion, the proper height relationship of chairs to tables, and all of the technical information and minutiae that factor into the way a room blends function and style and whether it all works together.

Take "one mirror per room." It's one of my favorite rules, and always comes immediately to mind. What I love about it is that it directs my thinking: it tells me to stop and to weigh all the options from every angle before making a decision. Of course you can have more than just one mirror in a room. Practically speaking, though, it's imperative to consider what the first mirror will do before even contemplating adding a second. Then it's critical to analyze what effect that second—or third, fourth, or fifth—will have. Will it reflect something it shouldn't? Will it create visual chaos? Will it add more light?

Design is a set of relationships, of interactions among objects, colors, patterns, textures, materials, and light—all with definite parameters. Through point and counterpoint, I strive for balance. Balance is everything. First I look at the big picture, the vision of what the room is supposed to be when it's finished. Then I choose the

individual elements, large and small, all of which affect each other and the room as a whole. A single object can bring the entire room into focus and cause everything else to fall into place.

I constantly review the impact of each decision on those already made and those still ahead. When matching a trim to a fabric, for instance, I evaluate its effect on the entire room—not just whether it goes with the fabric. How does it look with the chair behind it? With the wall color? The carpet? All these considerations factor into the end result.

I have always liked the comfort of order. When I was about to start high school, my family moved. After all those years with the nuns, it was total culture shock to be in a place that didn't require students to stand up or raise a hand when they wanted to ask a question. I had a hard time adjusting to the different rules, and to the fact that there were fewer of them. Like all new kids, I wanted to sit in the back of the room. The teachers put me in the front row, and I couldn't concentrate. I did poorly in algebra that year. But I retook the class, sat in the back, and did much better. What I discovered was that, with a little remove, I could always see how an equation balanced, and where the problem was when it didn't.

Over the years I've developed a kind of calculus of constants and variables that I use in my projects, in addition to applying the rules of design that I learned at the Fashion Institute of Technology, from other designers, and David Easton. For example, if a room's background— the paint job or the woodwork—is not perfect, everything will look second-rate. Never take shortcuts on the most crucial aspects of a project. Another golden design rule in my book is that good taste is impervious to trends. Still another involves the view: if it's good, open it up; if it's bad, cover it up. And always, always blend, never match—that's equally true for colors, styles, and proportions.

My list of personal rules contains only a few that I never bend, and they are relatively simple. Always keep passageways open. Too much furniture on one side of the room will throw off the balance. Furniture and carpets lined up with the room's perimeter tend to work better than those set on an angle—always be aware of where the diagonal points. Horizontal lines are restful. Vertical lines support structure. Too many curves look restless, but when used carefully they can balance the static effect of too many straight lines. Large-scale wallpaper? Heavy furniture pieces? Not in a small room. It's important to choose pieces that are as well-made as possible whether they are fine art or folk art. And too little is always, always, always better than too much.

As much as I love Cole Porter, and I do, I don't think "anything goes." The rules of design are like the rules of the road: they force you to be aware and to concentrate on what's happening around you. You ignore them at your peril. Yet there are design equivalents of jaywalking, which is rule-breaking at its best. The law may say to cross at the corner, but you know you can look left and right and make that choice of crossing mid-block for yourself. You shouldn't, but you do.

CARNEGIE HILL TOWNHOUSE

When space is tight, every area must serve a purpose—and sometimes more than one. That requires planning down to the last square inch. Working in advance, we were able to make this house, which architect Peter Pennoyer renovated beautifully for a young couple with two very small children, a paragon of efficiency.

The formal living room offers a good example. Intended for cocktail parties or after-dinner conversation, it now contains the desired three distinct seating groups and a grand piano—not an easy fit for the standard 20-foot width of a New York City brownstone. The family room, conversely, is arranged more casually, and meant for lounging—even sprawling—with deep sofas, comfy chairs, and ottomans.

An unusual multipurpose area—foyer, library, passageway, and dining room in one—connects the living room and family room. We lined it with bookcases, outfitted it with two inviting chaises, and found a library table that could serve triple duty as a desk, a place to stack art books, or a dining table. When the residents give a dinner party, they simply wheel the chaises into the elevator and surround the table, which becomes a central feature, with a complete set of Jacques Adnet chairs liberated for an evening from basement storage.

Silhouette and line move these clients as much as they do me—and so do pieces from the 1940s and 1950s. We love the same muted colors and the same balance of cool and warm hues. And they have a passion for the kind of detailing that separates the truly great from the merely nice, which made working with them a joy.

The André Arbus–designed, mid-twentieth-century, extendible library table—whose curving, X-shaped base mirrors the lines of the vaulting overhead—initiated the concept of converting this passageway into a multifunctional space. Chaises and shelves encourage its use as a library and occasional home office. On special occasions, it transforms easily to a formal dining room.

In the family room, the arch theme begun by Peter Pennoyer's architecture is echoed in the various curves of an early-twentieth-century Josef Hoffmann chair, a 1950s French chandelier, a 1940s French coffee table, and Jacques Adnet's c. 1950 desk. These combine to balance the room's more linear aspects, including the carpet's grid pattern. Leather, suede, and wool add texture.

Above and opposite: A small formal living room accommodates three separate seating groups through creative use of the corners. In one, a curved Davenport sofa floats at an angle and is fronted by a c. 1940 bronze Maison Jansen coffee table. The c. 1785 Hepplewhite bookcase displays family heirlooms. A custom banquette and a c. 1800 Japanese, lacquered storage box slip into another space.

A painting over the mantel appears to resemble a mirror that reflects the rest of the room back to the viewer, providing a wonderful glimpse of a far less tailored existence and making an intriguing, understated juxtaposition in the otherwise formal room. The silver pieces below are from the client's family's collection.

Above: Soft curves introduced by the chaise's curved back, the piano, the nineteenth-century Spanish marquetry table, the 1950s Spanish wall sconces, and the custom fabric of the curtains contrast subtly with the room's linear components. *Opposite:* Highly detailed pillow trims accentuate the room's other fine ornaments, including the side table's inlaid arabesques of exotic wood, bone, and mother of pearl.

PARK AVENUE COLLECTORS' APARTMENT

It may not be obvious to the casual observer at first glance, but function comes first in most if not all design decisions. Take this apartment: the clients are a young, fun couple with two adorable boys who love to run around and play basketball in the house. Recent transplants from London, they have a jazzy, sophisticated sense of color and a stunning collection of modern art from Asia—all of which affected the choices we made for the décor.

I don't always look at a client's art ahead of time, and I never choose fabrics to "go with" art because I don't want the one to blend into the other. Here, though, I knew the paintings were very bold, and that they could become completely overwhelming if the décor weren't just as robust. To create the necessary visual counterbalance, we opted for furniture with clear, strong lines, and for strong pattern elsewhere, especially underfoot.

The floor coverings came about in large part because of the boys. I had actually already done the apartment directly beneath this one for another client. When I was working on that project, I learned how much sound traveled through the ceiling because a family with boys lived upstairs then, too. My current clients wanted to make sure their family didn't disturb the neighbors, so to dampen the sound of boisterous children we put down two layers of carpet. The first, a wall-to-wall in chocolate brown, provides a great base for the second, the strongly patterned French, woven-wool zebra skin.

Pleats in the chair's fabric and the concentric squares of the mirror-framed mirror begin a theme of repeated linear, square, and rectangular elements that add pattern and texture to this living room.

High-contrast neutrals in the living room provide a strong but virtually colorless background for two haunting lithographs by Lin Tainmiao over the sofa. *Overleaf, left:* Pillows and books add the only splashes of strong color to the living room's essentially neutral palette. *Overleaf, right:* An assertive painting by Yin Jin in the family room, one of the pieces from the clients' collection of contemporary Chinese art, is balanced by equally bold décor.

ROCKY MOUNTAIN RETREAT

Context always plays a role in decorating, but not necessarily the role you expect. Take this six-bedroom vacation house in Aspen, for example. My clients use it both in summer and winter, so they needed the décor to span both seasons. That may not seem much of a challenge, but in Aspen, winter and summer are like night and day. Each element, every choice, had to walk a fine line: to make the rooms feel comfortable and cozy—read warm—for the winter, and comfortable—visualize cool—for the summer, too.

With its windowed expanses, the house embraces wonderful views of the surrounding Rockies. Taking cues from the beautiful natural environment, we used a tinted stucco treatment on the living and dining room walls. The creamy but not quite yellow shade reacts beautifully with the ever-changing light, and provides a warm background for the copper and earth tones that the clients love.

Given that they have four young children, this couple wanted to make sure that all the materials and furnishings would be kid-friendly and were not too precious to get actual use, which broadened our options. They did, however, insist on eschewing the hardy, all-season, lodge-style vernacular that's so prevalent here. Their taste, as I knew from previous projects together, tends to be refined and contemporary, like the architecture of this house and the modern art they collect. She particularly loves tactile fabrics and surfaces, and also has an eye for good twentieth-century furniture, as the Maison Jansen piece in the dining area demonstrates.

Furnishings united by a foundation of copper tones straddle seasons in this vacation home. Pattern and texture help to create intimacy in a large room, hence the choice of cut-velvet upholstery for the chairs, embroidered fabric for the ottoman, and an irregularly gridded carpet.

Contemporary twists on expected Aspen-style décor make this space feel fresh while acknowledging both the magnificent views and location. Tinted stucco feels cool in the summer and warm in the winter, and leaf patterns on the pillow fabric bring the outdoors in.

Above and opposite: Moss fringe on the suede sofa and deer embossed on the 1950s copper table lamps are the only obvious clues this room inhabits a Western setting; furniture with modern lines and a custom-designed carpet anchor it firmly in the present. *Previous pages, left:* The living room's mix of materials includes a bamboo-matting console table and an eighteenth-century Russian, gold-lacquered, iron-mounted steel trunk. *Previous pages, right:* Throughout the house, the ornate is balanced with the simple. Dressmaker details for the dining room chair slipcovers include a contrasting color for the skirt pleats and a button closure.

Above: In the bedroom, refined elements play off rustic cousins. The headboard and bed skirt are of cashmere, while the walls have a matte, dragged-paint finish that, dry and sheen-free, appears almost rough. Mirrored bedside tables add shine and a bit of glamour. *Opposite:* His-and-hers vanities are separated by a built-in tub that nestles into a niche to take advantage of the spectacular views; recessed blinds pull down when required. The tiles are glazed to resemble horn.

GREENWICH GUEST BEDROOM

Show house rooms are places for designers to experiment and to dream. Take this room, for example. I imagined it as a little guest bedroom waiting for me in London: just a bed, a place to sit, and a few simple, pretty things to please the eye.

I originally wanted and planned for upholstered walls and curtains. But show houses are nothing if not tests of a designer's improvisational skills. As the deadline for the opening approached, my upholsterers announced that they couldn't deliver the curtains on time—or cover the walls as planned. I was in a panic until I realized that Roman shades were quick to make, that backing linen fabric with paper and hanging it as wallpaper would be effective, and that my cabinetmaker—who did have time available—might be able to help me give the space some presence if I could devise an appropriate solution. That's when the idea for decorative wall panels came to me. I quickly located some fiberglass detailing molds, we built six panels, and used them to flank the windows.

When I'm working on a show house room, I'll often incorporate pieces of my own—the iron bed here for instance. The story goes that it once belonged to the decorator Michael Greer; one of my earliest purchases, it fit neatly into my old studio apartment. I still have it today. The color on the ceiling is one I particularly love—a very subtle blue with a tint of steel. The Lucite table is functional but adds a touch of whimsy and, most important, doesn't block the view through the room.

A 1940s Venetian mirror now in my house in Sharon and an eighteenth-century Swedish wall clock add personality and a sense of history to this show house room.

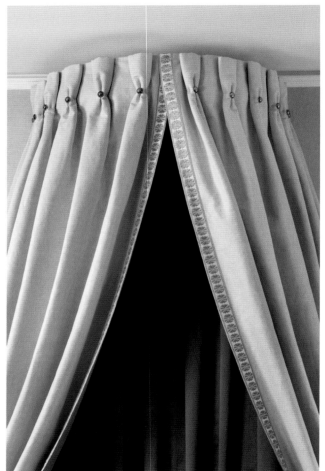

Above: Show houses, laboratories for designers, offer the opportunity to experiment with detail, as seen in the applied wall panels and the bed canopy here; both make the ceiling seem higher. *Opposite:* The Lucite table offers function and style without obstructing sight lines through the room. A carpet from my collection for Patterson, Flynn & Martin balances the detail above. *Previous pages:* Clean silhouettes and minimal ornament keep this space from feeling too decidedly feminine. The pale, cream-and-blue palette was inspired by the linen fabrics. The photos flanking the simple steel sleigh bed are by Lisa Fiel.

PLANS

Design is a domino effect: each decision affects every other decision. Floor plans, the most important planning tool in design, always drive the initial set of choices on every project, and all subsequent considerations refer back to it.

I look at a new space in two ways: for the architecture, and to get a sense of flow. Function comes first, so I want to know what purpose a room will serve—sleeping, eating, relaxing, entertaining—and whether the given dimensions suit the intended use. Is the space too large or too small, and if so, then what? My second concern is whether I can make that room accommodate the number of people who will move through it. Then come the essential elements: the ABCs of seating, wiring, lighting, storage, and so on. From there, my clients and I can decide what aspects of the design and décor to focus on first.

Because no two walls are the same and no two clients are alike, each floor plan is tailor-made to work for that client and that space. It's a diary of sorts: it shows whether the core lines up as it should, what options exist for placing the necessary elements, whether it's possible to add and subtract elements or move them around, whether people will be able to move easily and comfortably in and through the room once those elements are in place. A floor plan shows whether everything fits and, when it doesn't, whether it's possible to move a wall to solve a problem.

A CONNECTICUT COLONIAL REVISITED

There's something so twenty-first century about finding a Colonial-era house on the Internet, but that's how I came across this property. The farmhouse originally dates to the 1790s. Though successive additions, bad renovations, and a stint as an inn for lady schoolteachers had obscured the original, the best elements—the Palladian window, the tiger maple staircase with ivory inlay, and more—survived.

Restorations are always puzzles, but old houses can often tell you how they were meant to look if you listen. Follow the floorboards, and they'll show you what happened: paint and nails reveal what went up, what came down, and in what order. Take the staircase, for instance. Someone, sometime, had erected a wall against it, either to close it off or to back an upright piano, which actually served to protect the original wood from serious damage.

One afternoon during the demolition/construction process, I stopped by to see how things were coming. The place was in such disarray that I started to question the wisdom of buying it after all. I noticed that the brass chime on the front door was engraved with its patent date: September 8, 1848. September 8 is my birthday, so it seemed a sign that this was meant to be after all, and that I should stop complaining.

Furnishing the house was a practical business. I rummaged through the things I had in storage and developed the décor around pieces I already owned, mainly the furnishings from my former house in upstate New York supplemented by others I had purchased for former show houses. I painted the floorboards black, which tied everything in the house together. The collections? Favorite objects—precious as well as simple—picked up here and there over the years.

The core of this house dates to the late eighteenth century, as the facade reveals. *Overleaf:* Leftover show house pieces are put to work in the living room. The banquette was used at the Kips Bay Decorator Show House in 2001, as was the log box. The chairs were first used in an eBay show house.

Above and opposite: In the dining room, which doubles as a central hall, French chairs from the 1950s surround an extending table that holds a collection of objects. Maps of Paris form the backdrop. *Previous pages, clockwise from upper left:* An Irish Gothic chair, a favorite piece; a Robert Courtright study rests on a 1940s Argentine table; the front door's nineteenth-century doorbell patented on my birthday; the tiger maple banister; a portrait attributed to William Merritt Chase.

A room off the kitchen boasts an original beamed ceiling; the Dutch-doored extension dates to the 1940s or 1950s. The fireplace was given a new stone surround made by local stonemason Andy Savage. *Overleaf:* Many of these pieces, collected over the years, are linked by the common motif of leaves; most come from Trudy Weaver, an English dealer based in Notting Hill, London.

Reopening the upstairs landing uncovered a Palladian window, original glass intact. The carpet is one of my designs for Patterson, Flynn & Martin. *Overleaf:* A bedside table holds small amusements including a Robert Courtright collage, mementos of happy occasions such as place cards from a wonderful lunch, and items from places slated for future trips, like the ivory elephant from India.

Above and opposite: During the renovation, a warren of little rooms were converted into the master suite and guest room; the latter is over the kitchen and reached via the Colonial-era house's original stair. Landscape paintings cover the guest room walls. Plenty of places to sit are offered, including a 1960s Danish chair, as are plenty of books, like the volumes atop an early American chest. *Overleaf:* A guest bath with a claw-foot tub adds to the room's list of amenities.

PIED-À-TERRE ON FIFTH AVENUE

Some people feel that, to paraphrase the great Johnny Mercer, any place they hang up their hat makes that space a home. Others don't count a space as a home unless it has been tailored to reflect their particular tastes and needs. The latter is certainly the case with this two-bedroom pied-à-terre on Fifth Avenue. My client's principal residence is in Greenwich, Connecticut, but he wanted a comfortable, personalized place to stay when he's working at his office in the city. He also has two teenage sons who stay over regularly, and a big dog that's a full-time companion.

Comfort was key here, as was durability. He wanted all the upholstery to be deep enough and cushy enough to allow him and his boys to really sink into it. The sofa certainly fits that bill. The stone-topped coffee table is likewise essentially carefree: no one needs to worry if the boys put their feet up on it. To make sure the lounge chairs were proportioned properly, we based the design on a model from a men's club in London. The tailoring details—nailhead trim, contrasting tape on the hem of the sofa skirt—are classic and understated, and lend an air of sophistication to this garçonnière.

The mixture of grays and browns with splashes of red creates a handsome but not overly masculine environment. Furnishings and accessories hail from various pre- and postwar periods, including the 1940s and the 1960s. That particular mix actually suits the apartment, which is in the first residential building to go up on Fifth Avenue after World War II—but which has a definite prewar sensibility.

This apartment is tailored and masculine. The color palette tends to shades often found in menswear—grays and browns enlivened by jolts of red. The seating is ample in scale and designed for comfort; the lighting and accessories, simple but elegant.

The palette of grays, browns, and reds extends to art and accessories as well as fabrics. Understated upholstery details—tape, welting, nailhead trim—are modeled after fine tailoring. Objects from different decades reside harmoniously in the room, including bronze sconces from the 1940s, glass lamps from the 1960s by Nils Landberg for Orrefors, and French 1940s side tables of palissandre wood. Norman Bluhm's painting completes the space.

Above: The living room opens onto a terrace with a wonderful view of the Manhattan skyline.
In keeping with the tailored sensibility, the curtains are an unfussy combination of
fabric panels and Roman shades. The fabric-framed windowsill sets off two stone heads.
Opposite: A Robert Motherwell drawing hangs over a signed De Coene Frères–designed black
lacquer desk. Hailing from Brussels and dating to the 1930s, the desk also has a black leather
top and bronze pull; the black leather Jacques Adnet–style lamp has a brass tripod base.

Above and opposite: The apartment, although housed in a newer building, has a distinctively prewar feel. The master bedroom is composed of various shades of gray, with gray flannel at the windows and a darker gray flannel on the bed. The chair is upholstered in herringbone twill, continuing the menswear aesthetic. The carpet is a combination of wool and silk in a shade of anthracite. The dresser, an American design in ebonized walnut and brass from the 1950s, enhances the midcentury sensibility. A work by Byron Browne adorns the wall.

HORSE COUNTRY GETAWAY

When my clients purchased this converted stable as a family weekend house, it had a very baronial quality, with dark wood paneling everywhere—nice at night, but not as inviting in broad daylight. They're a younger couple with four children, three dogs, a rabbit, and hamsters. She's very tailored, loves to entertain, and does so quite a bit. They wanted sophisticated, straightforward rooms, rather than the stereotypical rustic barn conversion, for the kids and pets to romp in.

The original structure dates to the 1930s. Every owner since then had reconfigured it slightly, usually by tacking on another wing. We did the same, in the form of a kitchen addition and a separate pool house. Both have vaulted and trussed ceilings that mimic those in the living room. The other major structural change was in the dining room, where we incorporated French doors, which open to the patio beyond, to brighten the space.

The first thing we did was to paint the woodwork—though plenty of wood tone remains—which softened the effect of the paneling and made the rooms much lighter. Against that backdrop, we played with textures and tonal variation: brass next to cotton, leather adjacent to parchment, coco matting abutting silk. She loves Asian styles, and while their New York home takes a very formal approach to an Asian-fusion sensibility that mixes fine English antiques with superior Asian pieces, these rooms have a similar but more casual feeling created by Anglo-Indian tables, Eastern accents, and French furniture. Everything came new to the house, so we chose to emphasize graphic elements—especially circles, squares, and ovals.

Once an outbuilding on one of the area's great estates, this former stable was converted for residential use sometime in the first half of the 1930s. Subsequent owners repeatedly expanded the original structure with various extensions and wings.

The house's interiors were designed to be clean and light. Refinishing the existing woodwork with dragged paint was the first step in softening the space. *Overleaf:* A tone-on-tone palette emphasizes the play of textures, which includes a silk-bordered coco mat; a 1930s sycamore and vellum Gio Ponti table; cube-shaped, brushed brass side tables; leather upholstery; a cotton matelassé-covered sofa.

GREAT FRENCH PAINTINGS *from* THE BARNES FOUNDATION

Diana Widmaier Picasso PICASSO "Art Can Only Be Erotic"

PRESTEL

Large-scale pieces with bold silhouettes, such as a pair of Waldorf sofas and four teak tables with cast stone tops balance the architecture and tame the room's volume. Graphic effects—circles, squares, and ovals of various scales—establish visual order. *Overleaf:* Smaller-scale patterns such as the inlay on the nineteenth-century Indian octagonal tables and the appliqué and embroidery on the sofa pillows and the ottoman draw the eye at close range.

New French doors open the dining room to the terrace. Inside, comfortable, plush chairs beckon. The carpet has a silk field and coco mat borders, which help to tie the various spaces together while still differentiating them. The nineteenth-century, Qing dynasty sideboard expands the available storage space. The chandelier is French, from the 1960s.

Above and opposite: A newly constructed sitting area off the kitchen is glassed in on three sides and fitted with extremely comfortable lounge furniture. Inviting coppery tones, including the burnt orange fabric of the chairs and pillow fabric, prevail and brighten up this corner while relating to the neutrals used elsewhere in the project. The copper tabletop looks better the more it's used.

Above and opposite: These clients love to cook and entertain for neighbors and their own large family, so the kitchen was expanded to include a sun room large enough for a sofa, chairs, and a table that seats twelve. The new wing has vaults that mimic the original structure's; warm tones render the otherwise all-white kitchen homey.

Above and opposite: This master suite is a visual and physical oasis from the rest of the house—a place that's as simply decorated as possible so the mind can rest. A second-floor balcony overlooks the property. Fabrics are soft and fresh—wool challis, cotton, linen, and cashmere; each has a wonderful hand and a beautiful drape.

This two-story pool house is new construction, vaulted and trussed with reclaimed wood in the style of the original barn. The ceiling fixture, though contemporary, brings in a bit of the Art Déco feeling introduced in the main house. Its graphic themes—arches, curves, squares, and rectangles—are also present here.

COLOR

I love color. Yet color is so subjective and emotionally fraught that it can easily become a designer's stumbling block. There's no knowing what a certain shade may trigger in another's subconscious. What inspires me could depress someone else. Some people thrive in an interior dressed entirely in shades of gray, while others find it oppressive. Strong personalities often require strong backgrounds, and vice versa.

Clients tend to have very particular tastes in color and in pattern. One client, for example, loves a precise shade of rose. It can't have too much yellow. It can't have too much blue. It can't tend to coral, and it can't go peach. It has to be that just-so formulation, and she certainly knows—and reacts—when it's not. Another client can't abide anything with an avian motif: no birds, no feathers, no nests, no eggs, and absolutely no flora that looks remotely like it could be harboring chickadees, parrots, peacocks, or any other of the world's winged wonders.

When it comes to color and pattern, my goal is generally to narrow down palettes as far as possible—to pare them to their essential elements, to keep things simple. I've worked with clients, however, who have a passion for strong, saturated, difficult, even fauvist colors. I once created a space for a magazine in which the challenge was to incorporate as many patterns into a room as possible—I topped out at twenty-five fabrics. I wouldn't want to have to layer pattern on pattern or color on color so intensely all the time, but when cases arise that call for it,

The living room features a play of textures: leather, steel, and velvet, plus a loomed paper-and-wool carpet. The sheet steel mirror was commissioned based on a smaller version seen in a Greenwich Village shop; the artist makes them in his garage.

Above and opposite: The deep red walls in the living room were an experiment in color, and it took many coats of paint to get the red to just the right point of saturation. A painting by Charles Demuth found in an antique shop in upstate New York hangs over a Paul Frankl cork chest; the pieces atop it and to its right are finds from the Paris flea market.

Above and opposite: Line, silhouette, and form—the convex curves of an Eero Saarinen–inspired table base and the Chinese table leg, for instance—are juxtaposed in this space to draw attention to each other. *Previous pages, left:* A David Salle drawing in one corner of the living room is a particular favorite. Atop the table from Alpha Workshops is a model of the temple at Angkor Wat, which was carried back from Cambodia in a suitcase. *Previous pages, right:* The rare Van Day Truex male nude was a legacy from George O'Brien; the bookcase is Italian, from the 1960s.

Above and opposite: Objects serve as reminders of trips past and inspiration for trips yet to come: a sunburst mirror, an early flea market find, hangs above the bed; a scene from the 1933 Chicago World's Fair painted by Frederick Grant is positioned to its right; a sheer batik throw from Indonesia graces the bed; a bronze Poseidon plays a role in a fanciful vignette on a side table. *Overleaf:* A model of the Taj Mahal on the bedside table substitutes for an actual trip to India, for the moment. The bust of Benjamin Constant, the lover of Madame de Staël, was happened upon while reading his biography. The collage was a gift from Gloria Vanderbilt.

BEEKMAN PLACE GLAMOUR

As a designer, I welcome opportunities to continue learning. But some clients—this one in particular—have really pushed me to the limits of professional comfort. An extremely successful businesswoman who is glamorous and a bit larger than life, she was one of my first clients. She chose me for one simple reason: our aesthetics are polar opposites. As counterintuitive as that may seem, it is her standard operating procedure in business. She puts together project teams the same way, believing that the most successful results come when those with different—even opposing—viewpoints work in concert. Her preference is for bold, dramatic, personality-filled spaces, a far cry from the traditional, conventional, English-influenced schemes I had been putting together year after year—and which I showed her early in the design process. She repeatedly rejected them, encouraging me constantly to "take it up a notch," which certainly helped me break out of my mold.

Her duplex overlooks the East River, with wonderful water views on three sides. Because she's home only in the evenings and because she entertains frequently and on a large scale, she directed me to make the space shine at night. Passionate about color, she wanted the palette for the entire apartment to be derived from the multicolored glass panels in two remarkable antique brass lanterns she had found—and which we gave pride of place by installing in the entrance hall.

Reflective surfaces are everywhere: high-gloss finishes, an array of silk fabrics, accents of precious metals, materials with a slight sheen that catch the glimmer off the water and create a glow at night. She also loves the allure of French pieces from the 1940s—their dramatic lines complement the overall mood perfectly.

An aqua, stipple-glazed entrance hall announces this client's love of color. The apartment's entire palette was inspired by the 1940s Algerian lanterns' glass inserts. *Overleaf:* French Art Déco furniture, such as the rosewood-veneered 1930s table with scalloped edges that echo the banister's curves, plays a significant part in this space. Saturated hues balance bold patterns: Emile-Jacques Ruhlmann fabric covers a stool, a tiger-striped runner climbs the stairs, and a leafy bound-and-backed tapestry lies under the table.

Reflective materials make light dance for nighttime drama in the living room: the walls are of glazed, paint-covered, copper sheeting; mirrors surround the fireplace; and satin fabrics cover Knowle sofas. Scattered gilded accents, such as a pair of Austrian drop sconces from c. 1910 and the wheat sheaf base of a 1950s French coffee table enhance the glittering effect.

Above: Glass finials on window rods and gilded frames on French rope chairs add a subtle sparkle to the room. *Opposite:* A voluptuous 1925 Sue et Mare Cuban mahogany dining table and chairs—with their original leather—once belonged to Jean Renoir, the French film director, and were used in his house in Hollywood. *Previous pages, left and right:* A 1940s Jules Leleu rosewood bar with mother-of-pearl and fruitwood inlays is topped by a silvered Lucite and gilded brass light fixture.

Bold cobalt blue updates traditional paneling in the library. *Previous pages, left, clockwise from top:* A 1950s Venetian glass lamp; the mantel's lapis insert; an early-twentieth-century gilded bronze Austrian drop sconce; a 1950s French, glass-topped coffee table. *Previous pages, right:* A Fornasetti chair and burned velvet curtains have similarly shaped negative spaces.

Above: A c. 1940 sycamore veneer table by André Arbus and a curvaceous patent-leather-and-Lucite chair help the office compete for glamour with the rest of the apartment. A painting by Ross Bleckner hangs on the wall behind the desk. *Opposite:* In the kitchen, Robert Silvers's *James Dean*, 2003, dominates. The red-topped metal-like table and matching metal chairs by James Mont, c. 1940, add a steely sleekness.

KIPS BAY DECORATOR SHOW HOUSE

I'm the kind of designer who works best when there is a driving scenario or theme behind a project. When I do a show house, I often find myself creating a room either for myself or for a character that I can imagine living in that space. The story behind this beautifully proportioned, wood-paneled space on one of the show house's upper floors is a good example of that—and it was, as it happens, my first room for the Kips Bay Decorator Show House. Because a library, dining room, and living room already existed as the inventions of other designers working elsewhere in the house, I decided to create a self-contained retreat: a multipurpose bedroom that you wouldn't have to leave on Saturday mornings if you didn't want to, or that perfect place that you could come home to after work, shut the door, and just be happy to simply be out of the fray. There's a place to breakfast, a place to watch a little TV, a desk to work at, a chair by the fireplace—a little bit of everything.

The paneling, though lovely, absorbed so much light that the room desperately needed brightening. Wool sisal on the floor helps to lift the space, and red upholstery behind the bed adds a pop of color. One of the delights of doing a show house is that you can use furniture—in this case, fantasy furniture—that actual clients might find rather too much, like the Irish console here, which is carved with the face of a forest god straight from Celtic mythology. The nature of a paneled room is essentially classic and formal, though, and I wanted to honor that so I balanced the more whimsical elements with solid, recognizable pieces such as the klismos chairs with the Greek key detailing.

In a complex space, a piece in Lucite like this bedside table from the 1960s can calm the eye and still make a statement. A wonderfully soft, beautifully textured fabric upholsters the headboard and pops against the red wall. The Mexican mask was found in Santa Fe.

Above: A Jean Dubuffet hangs over a well-appointed bed. *Opposite:* English Regency klismos chairs add a classical touch to this formal, paneled room. The dining table was borrowed from my own apartment. *Overleaf, left:* A painting by Sewell Sillman, a protégé of Josef Albers, hangs above a wing chair and to the left of an antique cabinet on loan from Florian Papp. *Overleaf, right:* A unique Irish console, with its carved face straight out of Celtic mythology, pairs well with modern art.

Traditional Elegance in Westport

Traditional interiors require a particularly delicate balance. When they're overstuffed, they look old-fashioned. When they're underdressed, they look unfinished, like an unwelcoming hotel room. Each era of design has a balance between delicacy and heft, between minimalism and maximalism, that suits it best.

The eighteenth century probably provides the most enduring and widest variety of resources for bringing opposites into harmony. I look to it often. I certainly did here, where the great Irish manor houses provided a spark for the design. This was in part because my client is Irish and prefers classic, Anglo-hybrid styles and in part because of the nature of the house itself, which is new construction made to look old—just not as old as the client would have liked.

The first and most significant change we made involved the existing architectural details. The house had dentil molding everywhere, which to my client looked rather like giant teeth poised for attack. Because she loves woodwork though—lots of it—we replaced the original molding with a cleaner profile and added unfussy trim and wainscoting. The newly serene environment provided a fresh backdrop for all the traditional Anglo-Irish elements, such as her Staffordshire lions, without making them look too staid.

To inject some visual distinction into the blue-and-white sitting area off the blue-and-white bedroom—and to quiet the voluptuous effect of the curtains—we installed a version of the figured wall panels that I developed on the fly for an earlier Greenwich show house. They add both structure and ornament, just the solution we wanted.

The grand manor houses of Ireland inspired this interior. Architectural ornament, including wainscoting, crown molding, and paneling, are emphasized throughout. The wallpaper is an English print, and the striped stair runner has a strict geometry that works nicely with the strong lines of the banister and its spindles.

An inviting dining room by day also glows at night when light from a 1940s Murano-glass chandelier reflects off embroidered silk wall covering, a David Easton design. Furnishings range from nineteenth-century English styles to 1940s French, and a group of landscape paintings form the start of a collection. Silk-panel curtains with a beautiful trim finish the space simply.

Above: A little corner of the dining room harbors an abundance of detail and ornament: a carved mantel and intricate woodwork on a sideboard. *Opposite:* An upholstered, button-tufted banquette, which fits neatly into a niche, and an English, George II, tilt-top birdcage table, c. 1870, form a romantic spot for small dinners *à deux.*

Terra cotta–colored corduroy wallcovering creates a lively glow in the family room. The ottoman is large enough so children can stretch out on it and watch TV. *Overleaf:* Existing bookcases were reworked to keep woodwork detailing consistent. The room's decorative elements are classic Anglo-Irish, down to the Staffordshire lions and the English mahogany breakfast table.

Sky blue, a favorite color of the client, graces the bedroom and its adjacent sitting area. Softening and definition of the very high ceilings were achieved by the introduction of custom panels first experimented with at an earlier Greenwich show house. Striped curtains complete the feminine look.

Above: A guest room intended for guests of many sensibilities and ages is filled with comfortable furnishings and treats for the eye. The elements of the décor are traditional yet unfussy. *Opposite:* Use of the same carpet in both the sitting room and the master bedroom creates continuity between the two spaces. A change in wall covering and window fabric, however, indicates the transition from one to the other.

HISTORY

Here's another rule: never invest in a trend. If a new fashion should emerge that you just can't resist, go with it—but be prepared to change out whatever you buy soon thereafter. What's in tends to be out just as fast. If that all-the-rage piece or that must-have look isn't banished when its fifteen minutes of fame are up, the home and everyone in it will look sadly out of date.

Design and décor can and often do express aspects of our larger cultural preoccupations. This is no great revelation: we are influenced by where we grew up, what we grew up with, and by what we see and experience every day. What transports us emotionally can profoundly affect our ideas about the designs we want to live with. The places where we have had particularly memorable moments—great hotels, or restaurants, or favorite spots encountered in our travels—are terrific sources of inspiration for the kind of atmosphere we want to create at home. Movies and television also link sentiments with settings exceptionally well: think of *The Ice Storm*, for instance, *Brideshead Revisited*, or *The Jewel in the Crown*. Films or TV shows that evoke a period or an era captivate our visual imagination.

Our points of reference for imagining the rooms we would like to inhabit may have very little to do with an actual home, or a lot. A client once asked me to create an apartment interior based on the sets of *The Age of Innocence*, his favorite movie—a wonderful challenge. Other

MADISON AVENUE DUPLEX

As people enter new phases of their lives, they very often want to change their living spaces accordingly. That's the case here. Empty nesters now that their twin sons are out of the house, these clients opted for an apartment that was part of an estate sale and was spacious enough to accommodate frequent entertaining, large enough to show off their collections, and could welcome both sons home for short stays. Converted to a two-bedroom residence by James Joseph of Hottenroth + Joseph Architects, it suits their needs exactly.

Urban, sophisticated, and unpretentious, the interiors really reflect their occupants' style. Serious, passionate collectors from the first, they focus on pottery, on glass, and on fine art, editing as they continue to accumulate. With so many fine pieces in an apartment setting, however, the atmosphere needed to be curated carefully. The chandelier helps to "lighten" the mood in the living room: its embedded glass glitters whimsically but is still elegant enough to suit the gloriously proportioned space and the mix of furnishings.

Instead of an expected, formal dining room, we designated an area in the hallway adjacent to the kitchen for festive meals. A velvet-covered sofa framed by symmetrical floor-to-ceiling shelving serves the same purpose as banquette seating; additional chairs pull up to the table when needed. The guest room has twin beds, one for each visiting son. While the room is nicely appointed, it's not so lavish that it would encourage either to move back home!

Thanks to the architecture provided by tall, paned windows, this living room has all the glamour of New York in the 1940s. The ebony- and ivory-centered palette expresses the mood of that era and provides a great backdrop for the client's collections. The mix includes French 1940s polished brass étagères, a Chinese coffee table, late-eighteenth-century French bergères, and an antique French crystal-and-glass beaded chandelier.

Above: An ornate mirror adds sparkle. *Opposite:* The custom walnut-and-vellum cabinet's forceful lines pair well with a sweet Scottish bobbin chair. *Overleaf, left:* A dining area is carved out of an otherwise dead space in the hallway; its built-in bookcase displays Venetian glass. The tole-and-wood-beaded chandelier adds a note of indulgence. *Overleaf, right:* In the guest room, twin daybeds await visits from the clients' grown twin sons.

KENSINGTON HERITAGE

Every project comes with a unique client personality as well as the pieces the client has already amassed, extensive or not. Sometimes as a designer you fall into a trove of furnishings, accessories, art—all the elements of the interior to be. Sometimes it's necessary to purchase everything new. And sometimes, the client wants you to make the most of what's on hand for sentimental reasons, which is what happened here.

My client had inherited the family apartment—a great, rambling space with a terrace—the entire first level of a Kensington townhouse in London. Because the interiors hadn't been touched since Jon Bannenberg made them over for his parents when they purchased the flat in the 1960s, a major renovation was in order. The first steps focused on basics: upgrading the electrical systems, adding central air conditioning, and redoing the kitchen and floors. Once those were done, we worked on reorganizing his extensive possessions to create a newly harmonious mix.

The sorting, de-accessioning, and remixing of art, furniture, and accessories was daunting. The apartment was bursting with his parents' extensive collection of Renaissance art and fine English antiques. His personal passion is for Indian pieces, which also numbered in the dozens. Our objective was to edit and recombine parts of both collections into an environment that felt like it was truly his own. To lighten the atmosphere as well as to reduce the sheer number of pieces considerably, we gave many beloved—and any pieces the client felt neutral about—to other family members. He's now living comfortably and happily with this reconstituted collection. And he's still surrounded by the familiar pieces that keep his family's story alive.

In the foyer, the client's Indian art blends with Old Master paintings and furnishings he inherited. *Overleaf:* To make the apartment look and feel modern, pieces with subtle sympathies but vastly different provenances were paired; the table leg relates to the fireplace, for example.

The unusual placement of a narrow carpet stretched across a room works for this unusually large space; half functions as the living room, the other half as the library. The coffee table is a Chinese daybed inset with cane. A tapestry fabric covers antique Georgian chairs. *Overleaf, left:* Pattern abounds in the apartment, as a close-up of this Turkish Iznik plate suggests. *Overleaf, right:* In the office off the bedroom, I crowned the bookcase with a gilded pelmet that belonged to the client's parents; for many years it held portières that hung, like doors, between two rooms of the apartment.

Above and right: The client saw this early-nineteenth-century dining table in a second client's home, professed an admiration for it, and when the second client moved, it became his. A Gustav Klimt study for a theater safety curtain hangs over the room's console. Built-in shelving was painted black to show off a collection of Indian silver. Pierced stone screens found at a London art gallery modulate the light.

This client has a wonderful eye, and loves to look for beautiful things wherever he travels; we often spend Saturday mornings on Portobello Road as well, and the apartment is filled with finds from those visits. A Renaissance library table holds a collection of these objects, including a Chinese jade scholar's rock and an antique porcelain bust. His mother made the carpet.

Believing that his offer on this
eighteenth-century Moghul, tripartite
facade was for only one section,
the client was stunned when the full
piece arrived intact, and we quickly
extended the platform intended to hold
the smaller section as a headboard.

TWIN LAKES FARM

When these clients, who have young children, fell in love with this long-abandoned, early-nineteenth-century Connecticut farmhouse and decided to transform it into their weekend getaway—and a working dairy farm—it was bordering on collapse. In its recent past, the place had belonged to Bing Crosby's brother; purportedly Bing and his wife visited when Bing's wife was doing a play at nearby Williamstown.

Our renovation was soup to nuts: stripping the original house to its studs and demolishing the unsightly additions; refitting the surviving structure with new electrical, plumbing, and roof; replacing the property's concrete fence with a classic stone wall; repairing the existing floors; rebuilding the chimneys; restoring the original details; and reusing as many rehabbed fixtures, such as original bathtubs and mirrors, as possible.

These clients have traditional but unfussy taste so I pared ornament to the minimum. Instead of big window treatments, simply trimmed linen panels hang in the ground-floor fenestration. Walls painted to match the drapery fabric make for very quiet, light-filled rooms. The couple loves antiques so the challenge here was mainly finding the right pieces, preferably in or from the surrounding area, which has a long, well-documented furniture-making tradition. Because I'm driven by a sense of line both literal and metaphorical, I often find myself drawn to pieces for their silhouettes as much as for their stories. That was certainly the case here, and to me it makes sense since I find traditional furniture—and particularly American antiques—to be as visually compelling as those of contemporary design.

The original farmhouse dates to c. 1810. *Overleaf:* Intense light from so many large windows is allowed to become the living room's main color. Signed Jones of Ruthin, a c. 1800, George III case clock with a beautiful chime graces a nook between two windows. Victorian mahogany makes partners of a desk and chair, both c. 1880, that fit neatly into a bay window.

A triptych from the client's photography collection graces the wall above the sofa and establishes the entire room's color palette. The early-twentieth-century French brass-and-leather coffee table, nineteenth-century walnut-and-burl inlaid side table, and the c. 1800 English two-drawer side table with ivory and reeded legs contribute to the paired-down, traditional look.

Separated by a hallway from the living room, the dining room is its mirror image. The curves of the David Duncan English mahogany dining table, neoclassical mahogany chairs, early-twentieth-century Flemish chandelier, and demilune tables help to soften the room's boxy and long proportions. The fireplace's beautiful oval medallions are echoed by the nineteenth-century painted and parcel gilt oval mirror.

Above: Another photographic triptych by the same photographer whose work appears in the living room hangs over an English mahogany cabinet with a shaped gallery top, c. 1830, that adds curve to the living room. The bobbin chairs contribute curves of another scale. *Opposite:* Certain traditional, eighteenth-century forms feel quite modern in their minimalism.

Above: The master bedroom's tall post bed dates to c. 1850. To create consistency, every room is painted linen white; panels of the same fabric also hang in all the windows except for the bedroom's, where the fabric is one of my designs for Schumacher. A housewarming gift, the needlework picture features a mountain that closely resembles those visible from the house. *Opposite:* The dressing room contains a nineteenth-century dressing table and a mid-nineteenth-century inlaid barometer.

Living with Art

Connecticut country with a sense of humor? Why not? If this house took itself too seriously as far as décor goes, it wouldn't suit the couple whose weekend getaway it is. They are light, happy, and fun. They love color. She's a wonderful cook, and they entertain often.

The guiding principle here was comfort, which is as much a psychological issue as a physical one. Here's why: I think every room should function for a single occupant as well as it does for a group. That takes planning. The volumes of this house are generous, so I organized the furniture to create both intimate spots for people to curl up in by themselves and to sit with friends. Adding color, detail, texture, and pattern to the corners ensured that there was plenty to look at from any vantage point, which also helps make the far reaches of the room seem not so very far after all.

This house has an interesting combination of rustic and refined elements attributable to the husband's love of industrial design. He haunts local antiques shows and flea markets, which is the origin of many of the small objects—the mechanical toys, for instance—that give the rooms such a sense of whimsy. This client and I have a ritual: the Saturday morning of every Memorial Day and Labor Day, we go to the Rhinebeck Antiques Fair. The dealers can see that we are looking for something unexpected. You never know what will strike my client's fancy—last time, he purchased an entire collection of antique chocolate molds.

Design decisions for this Connecticut farmhouse were driven by the clients' art collection and their desire that the interiors have a true "country" feel. The strong imagery is balanced by equally forceful pattern and color used in moderation. The painting is by Carroll Dunham.

Above and opposite: Bold forms introduced by the wing chair and sofa plus soft textures in neutral colors and tone-on-tone patterns make for a very comfortable living room. The pair of Scottish armchairs date to the 1940s. The area rug is made of hemp. The large wood sculpture is by Bryan Nash Gill, and the photo over the sofa is by Laurie Simmons. *Overleaf:* An antique American table stands over an antique American painted chest in the entry hall. The two were paired for the sympathy between their rustic wood colors, and the mirror was added to the vignette for the way its frame echoes the shape of the table legs. The carpet is by Elizabeth Eakins.

Above and opposite: That the room's rug and the wall sculptures mirror each other closely is a case of life emulating art: the rug design preceded the art in this case—an assemblage of rulers by John Salvest—because of its year-long lead-time for delivery. *Previous pages:* A custom dining table made by a Brooklyn artisan who crafts furniture out of former railroad ties and other pieces of track; its weight dictated the installation of a steel beam in the floor for support. The custom ebony Windsor chairs are a touch of historic Connecticut, and pair well with the table's simple lines. The installation of butterflies is by Paul Villinski.

Above and opposite: That the room's rug and the wall sculptures mirror each other closely is a case of life emulating art: the rug design preceded the art in this case—an assemblage of rulers by John Salvest—because of its year-long lead-time for delivery. *Previous pages:* A custom dining table made by a Brooklyn artisan who crafts furniture out of former railroad ties and other pieces of track; its weight dictated the installation of a steel beam in the floor for support. The custom ebony Windsor chairs are a touch of historic Connecticut, and pair well with the table's simple lines. The installation of butterflies is by Paul Villinski.

Above: The toile-patterned wall covering in the master bedroom features scenes of deer in the woods, a contextual reference to the house's country setting. The antique bed is of tiger maple and has a tulip top. *Opposite:* The upstairs landing displays some of the client's collections, including Robert Rauschenbergs on the wall and antique whirligigs on the bench. The custom carpet is by Elizabeth Eakins.

DETAILS

I love whimsical objects. I have pieces, usually vintage items or antiques, which I couldn't resist buying because I found them amusing. One recent purchase was an old, handmade, Danish butter mold. It serves absolutely no purpose whatsoever: who uses a turned-wood butter mold these days? Yet I get great pleasure from the feel of it in my hands and from thinking about how it must have worked. Other objects, such as a temple stone I brought back from a trip to Angkor Wat, hold special meaning for me. As much as I love to have these little treasures around me, clutter drives me crazy. So when the infatuation has passed and the sentiment has faded, I'll either put some of my pieces away for awhile—I rotate things in two-year cycles—or get rid of them altogether to keep the décor looking clean and fresh.

Many of us collect, but first-edition folios, twentieth-century glass, eighteenth-century silver snuffboxes, outsider art, etcetera, can amass quickly in a space, to the point of making it overflow. Because too much storage space is never enough, most interiors need a regular attitude adjustment—a ruthless edit to pare down the unnecessary details. I do this for myself, and I happily do it for longtime clients, too. One couple, for instance, called recently because they were overwhelmed by their living room. I designed their house years ago, but hadn't been back in at least a decade. This couple travels frequently, and they always bring back wonderful mementos from each trip. As a result, and almost without their being aware of it, the space for relaxing and entertaining had

become overstuffed with souvenirs. I sent them out for a few hours while I combed through the room shelf by shelf, surface by surface, filling a laundry basket with things that seemed out of context. When they came back, they were much happier: the visual chaos was brought to order, and they couldn't even tell what I had removed.

How we edit depends on the ways in which our individual eyes have been trained. There are many ways to cultivate a sense of discernment; the camera helped me develop mine early. Just after college, I was working as a photographer in upstate New York, mostly documenting horse farms—both the architecture and the horses. One of my projects involved recording the architectural details on older buildings—cupolas, shutters, moldings, and so on—for the Goshen Historical Society. That need to compose within a frame, to see line and silhouette and the interplay between them, has definitely informed what I do.

The best rooms are more than just a pleasing and appropriate sum of form, color, texture, pattern, and light—the conventional and essential elements of décor. My favorite rooms are rooms where every single object either has meaning, or at least are filled with objects that lend themselves to having fictional narratives invented about them! Rooms such as these contain nothing extra, nothing too much, nothing brought in just to fill an empty space. Some of the furnishings may show a sense of humor. Others may express a facet of personality or family history. Everything is lived in and loved and evokes a remembrance of something, someone past.

Perhaps that's why I still find so much inspiration in the English country house style, which is eclectic in the very best sense of the word. For all their grandeur and excess, none of the great English country houses is

self-conscious. The people who built them traveled the world. They brought pieces of the Empire home. They thought about the provenance of each piece, and were highly discerning about where they placed their finds and how they used them. Touring these rooms—or just poring over photographs of them—immediately brings to mind a portrait of the individuals who sank into those sofas, and the dogs that flopped obediently at their feet.

The line between pretension and everyday opulence is fine, and the degree of comfort offered by a room that could go either way is often the differentiating factor. The rooms of the great English country houses still exemplify casual luxury: it's evident that people lived comfortably in them then and could live comfortably in them now. Even in the grandest of those very elegant rooms, the foundations of livable design are there. There is always a lamp to read by, a convenient place to put a drink, a table at the perfect height to receive a tea tray. Pictures, portraits, and personal artifacts provide a sense of history—layers upon layers of history, actually. The furniture and objects have a sense of lightness, no matter how heavy they are, and a sense of quirkiness. Even that enormous and ever-present Bridgewater sofa, which we take for granted now as part of the English tradition, must have looked contemporary in its day.

The life in those houses comes from the layering of details and elements added by successive generations, which is what I think makes these rooms look as if their families are still at home. Perhaps that's why I still believe in the concept of the "grand tour." The objects that we choose to bring into our homes from the places that we visit, and also from those that we have not yet seen, please our eyes, trigger our memories, and, best of all, occupy our imaginations.

A PARK AVENUE CLASSIC

Every interior can reach a point of perfect equilibrium, a balance that reflects the individual personalities of its occupants and their nature as a couple or a family. This project, due to the wonderful working relationship I developed with the clients, reflects that much-sought-after sense of order. The wife has a design professional's sense of scale, proportion, line, and color. She also knows a lot about and appreciates fine furniture and objects because she's grown up with them: her grandmother had a wonderful collection of English furniture, and so do her parents. A major collector of contemporary art himself, the husband also hails from a family of serious collectors. Here he makes decisions about the art, she tends to the furniture and fabrics, and it all works for their lifestyle, four young children, and a significant amount of entertaining.

Because the architecture is so strong, and because each piece we selected has its own clear merit, we didn't feel the need to fill in every last square inch of space. The mix is lively, ranging from Scottish Regency to eighteenth- and nineteenth-century English to 1940s and 1950s pieces like the living room's mirrored coffee table.

She likes the formal and the casual in juxtaposition, as illustrated by the window treatments in the living room. The detailing? Swags, jabots, and molded tassels. Yet the ultratraditional drapes are made of the most ethereal wool challis, an altogether modern fabric. Had she chosen damask, taffeta, or satin, the effect would have been too stuffy. Rendered in wool, however, the curtains take on the look of a Geoffrey Beene dress—at once couture and contemporary. That attitude pervades the décor. So while it's clear that this is the apartment of a sophisticated, modern couple, it has furniture that even a grandmother would love.

This city dining room could easily be in an English country house filled with furniture and art accumulated over generations. Aubergine walls show off an early-seventeenth-century Japanese screen from Galerie Ariane Dandois as well as the nineteenth-century Regency dining table and chairs and the c. 1920 crystal chandelier.

Above: A fine George III mahogany console, c. 1790, and a Josef Albers painting grace a wall. *Opposite:* A late-eighteenth-century Scottish mantel inspired the room's faux-stipple woodwork and aubergine walls. *Previous pages, left:* Floral and vine motifs delicately wind their way from mantel to console, silver chalice, and Bagues sconce from the 1940s. *Previous pages, right:* Understated fabrics, such as the chairs' muted stripes and the harlequin carpet, add subtle pattern to the room. The c. 1770 George III armchairs are attributed to Thomas Chippendale.

The living room blends twentieth-century pieces, such as a 1950s French mirrored coffee table, with eighteenth-century English pieces. Each item has its own merit, from the George III secretary to Josef Hoffmann's fluted silver candlesticks. *Overleaf, left:* A George III marble-topped console from Kentshire Galleries sets the tone for the entry. *Overleaf, right:* At the windows, traditional style and classic ornaments meet modern couture fabrics.

In this couple, she knows and appreciates fine furniture and fabrics, he knows and collects art, and they're both equally engaged in creating their home. The muted palette and discreet tone-on-tone use of pattern create a fitting background for their extensive collection of contemporary art, which includes a Philip Guston over the living room sofa.

THE FRENCH CONNECTION

Some clients know exactly what they wish their homes to become, and they spend their lives in a state of reverie envisioning them—and the atmosphere—down to the last nuanced detail until the time comes when they have the opportunity to make the dream a reality. This client is one of that rather rare breed. A Francophile to her fingertips, she adores French furniture and decorative arts from all periods. She has a particular passion for Art Déco, which was her style of choice for the dining room. And she collects French art, especially paintings and drawings of the late nineteenth and early twentieth centuries.

The place that she had been dreaming of re-creating in apartment form? The legendary Hôtel Ritz on the Place Vendôme in Paris, where she vowed to live one day after seeing photographs of it as a child. So it was logical that we would stay there for inspiration when we flew to Paris to shop for this apartment. During that one trip, we purchased almost everything for these interiors, which are entirely French except for a few good pieces for variety that you can count on one hand: a pair of nineteenth-century Italian gilt armchairs from Florian Papp, an early-nineteenth-century English carpet, an antique Spanish mirror, and a Chinese dragon.

She also had her color palette firmly in mind: the pinks, the reds, and the blues that she's always favored. It's not the easiest task to mix warm tones with cool colors and make them work together harmoniously, but it was definitely fun to do so with her favorites here—especially because the palette is so very flattering for her.

This client is a lifelong Francophile and admires Art Déco, as her 1930s René Prou cabinet shows. *Overleaf:* French pieces from various periods and styles combine to give an overall impression of glamour while allowing "outsiders" such as Chinese porcelain, c. 1760 Italian gilded armchairs, and a late-eighteenth-century English Axminster carpet to blend in. Pinks, reds, and blues unite the space.

Above and opposite: Upholstered walls envelope a dining room suite of Art Déco furnishings by Eric Bragge, a jewelry designer as well as an architect. Leavening of the heady style statement is accomplished by inclusion of a mid-nineteenth-century English Axminster rug, an antique Spanish mirror, and silver lamps and candlesticks.

WEEKENDS IN PARIS

Rome gets all the attention in the saying about the value of adapting yourself to your surroundings, but as a designer, the allure for me has always been to see if I could pull off a space that felt absolutely, authentically Parisian. As soon as I decided to keep a place there, I knew I wanted it to look and feel like the perfect distillation of a French interior.

This is the very first apartment I looked at, and I fell in love with it immediately. It's in the sixth arrondissement, on the third floor of a building said to have belonged to Voltaire. The location couldn't be more perfect: there's history—and many neighborhood antique stores! Plus the Louvre and the Musée d'Orsay are within easy walking distance. The rooms retain their perfect, eighteenth-century proportions. They are also flooded with natural light, and the apartment's iconic original ornaments, including Versailles-patterned parquet floors, gilt-trimmed paneling, a marble mantel, and wrought-iron window railings are intact.

Given the commute, I knew I did not want to have every forthcoming trip taken up with decorating the apartment bit by bit. So I focused, and dedicated a twenty-four-hour shopping spree to accumulating furnishings and accessories. On Wednesday of that week, the apartment was empty. The delivery truck showed up on Friday, and I had a cocktail party that night.

Rooms of this era show off a mix of modern and period pieces just beautifully, so that's what I opted to use here. The Philippe Starck designs—steel bookcase, plastic table, and slipcovered desk chair—look right at home with the Frédéric Méchiche chaise, the Louis XVI leather armchair, and the small Chinese table I picked up at the Porte de Clignancourt flea market.

Every corner of this apartment has a designated function. On the Philippe Starck–designed dining table are masks by Robert Courtright, a favorite artist. The gilded trumeau mirror is original to the apartment, and probably dates to the late eighteenth century. The stool is by Bruno Romeda.

A view of the living room through to the bedroom shows furnishings of mixed periods, all of which were purchased either in the flea market or in stores on the Left Bank. Three Josef Albers prints hang over the daybed. The andirons are of my design. A bronze bust of Hades keeps watch over the bedroom's secretaire.

Above and opposite: Philippe Starck pieces look and feel at home here, in period architecture and next to Albers prints—they repeat the motif of square geometry at different scales that is underlined by the Frédéric Méchiche chaise. The sofa under the mirror converts to a bed to accommodate guests.

The rooms of this apartment are
flooded with light, thanks to the
eighteenth-century fenestration. All
the architecture, ornament, parquet
flooring, and gilded detailing are
original to the interior—and so is
the walk-in closet beside the alcove
that houses my bed. A Philippe
Starck chair pulls up to the
secretaire and a Chapoval painting
hangs beside the closet door.

ACKNOWLEDGMENTS

Special thanks to Stacee Gravelle Lawrence and Andrea Monfried of The Monacelli Press for green lighting this project and making it all happen.

To Jill Cohen, my agent, I bless the day Dan Shaw gave me your number!

To Doug Turshen and Judith Nasatir for making me look and sound so good.

To John Gruen and Raina Kattleson for long creative days shooting across the country.

I would like to thank Gerald Pushel and the design teams of Schumacher and Patterson, Flynn & Martin. Especially Susan North, Honore Buckley, Liz Nightingale and Mason Morjikian.

I especially want to thank my favorite architects Peter Pennoyer, Jim Joseph, and John Murray for creating perfect spaces to work on.

Thanks to Annie Kelly, Florence de Dampierre, Tim Street-Porter and Wendy Goodman, who encouraged me over lunch last spring to do this book. Beth Daugherty for her expert advice, and Mike Strohl who first came up with the idea.

To Susan Becher, Jeffrey Brody, Alexis Contant, Janice Langrill, Dennis Lee, Peter Margonelli, Mindy Papp, Deborah Rathbun, Jane Schott, and Rachel Webster. Thank you for long-term professional support and friendship.

Also many thanks to someone I promised to take to the Cloisters before a big birthday. No rush as the invitation is always open and you will always be 39 to me! I value our friendship and your loyalty.

Special thanks to Karen Howes at The Interior Archive, as well as to The Aspen Branch and Harper and Toms for their beautiful flowers.

To my sisters Lorraine and Eileen and aunts Catherine Ruquet and Eileen Kent for many years of encouragement and support.

I would like to thank the Kips Bay Decorator Show House for giving me the chance to first present my work to the public. Sincere thanks to the Kips Bay board, Pat Carey, Harry Hinson and the late Rella MacDougall.

Finally, sincere thanks to Gloria Vanderbilt for reminding me to always look for positive viewpoints both professionally and personally.

PHOTOGRAPHY CREDITS

Principal photography by John Gruen and David Todd. Styling by Raina Kattelson.

Courtesy Elle Décor Magazine/Corbis Images and Fernando Bengoechea: 231, 232–33, 234, 235, 236–37

Peter Margonelli: 9, 48–49, 141, 142, 143, 144, 145, 161, 165, 166, 167, 168, 169

Courtesy Traditional Home Magazine and Bruce Buck: 47

Simon Upton: 6, 171, 172, 173, 174–5, 176, 177, 178, 179, 180–81, 182–83
    Styling by Caroline Englefield

Library of Congress Cataloging-in-Publication Data
Smyth, Matthew Patrick.
Living Traditions : Interiors by Matthew Patrick Smyth. — First edition.
p. cm.
ISBN 978-1-58093-309-4 (hardcover)
1. Smyth, Matthew Patrick—Themes, motives. 2. Interior decoration—United States. I. Title.
NK2004.3.S64A4 2011
747.092—dc22   2010044522

Printed in China

10 9 8 7 6 5 4 3 2
Second edition

www.monacellipress.com
Design by Doug Turshen with Steve Turner